Learning Short-take®

UNDERSTANDING AND MANAGING
DIVERSITY

Manager and employee toolkit for an inclusive workplace

CATHERINE MATTISKE

TPC - The Performance Company Pty Ltd
PO Box 639
Rozelle NSW 2039
Sydney, Australia

ACN 077 455 273
email: info@tpc.net.au
Website: www.tpc.net.au

© TPC – The Performance Company Pty Limited
Publication date: April 4, 2011

All rights reserved. Apart from any fair dealing for the purposes of study, research or review, as permitted under Australian copyright law, no part of this publication may be reproduced by any means without the written permission of the copyright owner. Every effort has been made to obtain permission relating to information reproduced in this publication.

The information in this publication is based on the current state of commercial and industry practice, applicable legislation, general law and the general circumstances as at the date of publication. No person shall rely on any of the contents of this publication and the publisher and the author expressly exclude all liability for direct and indirect loss suffered by any person resulting in any way from the use of or reliance on this publication or any part of it. Any options and advice are offered solely in pursuance of the author's and the publisher's intention to provide information, and have not been specifically sought.

National Library of Australia
Cataloguing-in-Publication data

Mattiske, Catherine
Understanding and Managing Diversity: Manager and Employee Toolkit for an Inclusive Workplace

ISBN 978-1-921547-24-9

1. Occupational training 2. Learning I. Title

370.113

Printed in USA

Distributed by TPC - The Performance Company - www.tpc.net.au
For further information contact TPC - The Performance Company, Sydney Australia on +61 9555 1953 or TPC - The Performance Company, California on +1 818-227-5052, or email info@tpc.net.au

HELLO.

Welcome to the Learning Short-take® process!

This Learning Short-take® is a bite sized learning package that aims to improve your skills and provide you with an opportunity for personal and professional development to achieve success in your role.

This Learning Short-take® combines self study with workplace activities in a unique learning system to keep you motivated and energized. So let's get started!

Step 1:
What's inside?

- Learning Short-take® Participant Guide. This section contains all of the learning content and will guide you through the learning process.
- Learning Activities. You will be prompted to complete these as you read through the Participant Guide.
- Learning Journal. This is a summary of your key learnings. Update it when prompted.
- Skill Development Action Plan. Learning is about taking action. This is your action plan where you'll plan how you will implement your learning.

Step 2:
Complete the Learning Short-take®

- Learning Short-takes® are best completed in a quiet environment that is free of distractions.
- Schedule time in your calendar to complete the Learning Short-take® and prioritize this time as an investment in your own professional development.
- Depending on the title, most participants complete the Learning Short-take® from 90 minutes to 2.5 hours.

Step 3:
Meet with your Manager/Coach

- Schedule a 30 minute meeting with your Manager or Coach.
- At this meeting share your completed Activities, Learning Journal and Skill Development Action Plan.
- Most importantly, discuss and agree on how you will implement your learning in your role.

Welcome

Understanding and Managing Diversity
Manager and Employee Toolkit for an Inclusive Workplace

Understanding and Managing Diversity provides you with specific skill development in either managing or contributing to an inclusive and diverse workplace through understanding and displaying acceptable workplace behaviors. It includes general guidelines and information, underpinned by specific legislation relating to workplace conduct (discrimination, harassment, bullying, and victimization) in most countries.

Developing and maintaining an inclusive and diverse workplace is not just about complying with the legislative and organizational code of conduct requirements. What's just as important is that everyone in the workplace displays respectful behavior, which is inclusive and reflects the values of fairness and equal opportunity for all.

Understanding and Managing Diversity will develop your skills in balancing the application of relevant legislation and Code of Conduct policies in the workplace with displaying acceptable workplace behaviors of respect, fairness and transparency in all interactions.

Understanding and Managing Diversity includes the **Defining Workplace Behavior Job Aid**, provided as a free downloadable tool.

Now let's get started!

1	Participant Guide > Start here
2	Learning Journal 79
3	Skill Development Action Plan 85
4	Quick Reference 91
5	Next Step 113

> "Preconceived notions are the locks on the door to wisdom."
> Merry Browne

"Our thoughts are unseen hands shaping the people we meet. Whatever we truly think them to be, that's what they'll become for us."

Richard Cowper

Section 1

PARTICIPANT GUIDE

Start here

What's in this Participant Guide

"The highest result of education is tolerance."

Helen Keller

Table of Contents

How to Complete Your Learning Short-take®	5
Activity Checklist	6
Learning Objectives	7
Let's Get Started	8

Part 1 - Inclusion and Diversity — 9
What is an Inclusive and Diverse Workplace? — 11
The Business Case for Diversity and Inclusion — 14
The Risks — 16
Implementing Diversity — 21

Part 2 - Locating Policies and Legislation — 23

Part 3 - Workplace Discrimination — 29

Part 4 - Workplace Harassment — 35
Sexual Harassment — 37
Bullying — 41
Victimization — 59

Part 5 - The Inclusive and Diverse Workplace in Action — 65
Building a Diverse and Inclusive Workplace — 66
Guidelines for Behaving in a Respectful, Fair and Transparent Manner — 69

Part 6 - Impact, Prevention and Taking Action — 73
Impact of Unacceptable Workplace Behavior — 74
Obligation and Prevention — 75
Taking Action against Physical or Verbal Harassment — 76

How to Complete your Learning Short-take®

1. **Reflect on your skills and abilities** in managing or contributing to an inclusive and diverse workplace through legislative knowledge and displaying acceptable workplace behavior.

2. **Complete the initial skills assessment.**

3. Highlight specific skill areas that you believe you could develop more. Add these to the **Learning Journal**. Add to your Learning Journal as you go.

4. When you have completed this Learning Short-take® **meet with your Manager/Coach.** In this meeting, you will jointly establish a personal **Skill Development Action Plan.**

5. **Subject to your coach's final review** and assessment, you will either sign off the module, or undertake further skill development as appropriate.

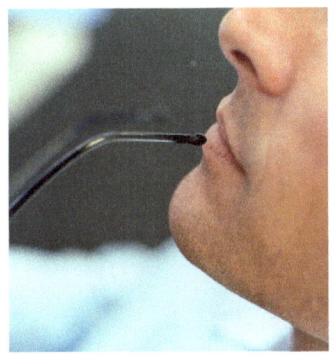

"Kindness is the language which the deaf can hear and the blind can see."

Mark Twain

Activity Checklist

1

"Courage is fire, and bullying is smoke."

Benjamin Disraeli

During this Learning Short-take® you will be prompted to complete the following activities:

- Activity 1 -   Initial Skills Assessment   12
- Activity 2 -   Benefits and Risks in a Diverse and Inclusive Workplace   18
- Activity 3a - Organizational Definition Search   25
- Activity 3b - Regional Definition Search   27
- Activity 4 -   Discrimination Case Study   33
- Activity 5 -   Sexual Harassment Case Study   39
- Activity 6 -   Bullying Case Study   50
- Activity 7 -   Cyber Bullying Case Study   57
- Activity 8 -   Victimization Situations   61
- Activity 9 -   Respect Fairness and Transparency   71
- Activity 10 - Grievance Procedure   78
- Learning Journal   79
- Skill Development Action Plan   85

Disclaimer: This Learning Short-take® does not constitute legal information or legal advice, nor should it be used in any manner that is connected to a workplace employment claim and should not be relied upon as such and merely conveys general information related to issues commonly encountered in the workplace. Although the author goes to great lengths to make sure our information is accurate and useful, it is recommended that you consult a lawyer if you want professional assurance that our information or your interpretation of it is appropriate to your particular situation. The publishers of this Learning Short-take® are not engaged in rendering legal advice. This Learning Short-take® is not meant to provide a comprehensive picture of any particular situation and you are strongly encouraged to seek counsel for interpretation or a course of action.

Learning Objectives

After you have completed this Learning Short-take®, you should be able to:

- Explain the importance of an inclusive and diverse workplace to business.
- Define what is meant by an inclusive and diverse workplace.
- Define different types of unacceptable behavior in the workplace i.e. harassment, discrimination, victimization and bullying.
- State the responsibilities of employees and managers in ensuring an inclusive and diverse workplace for all.
- Examine case studies dealing with discrimination, sexual harassment, bullying, Cyber bullying and victimization.
- Define and identify three examples of the behaviors of respect, transparency and fairness in the workplace that you can develop which will contribute to a diverse and inclusive workplace.
- Identify and list where to go for help if confronted by unacceptable behavior in the workplace as defined in this Learning Short-take®.

"If we cannot now end our differences, at least we can help make the world safe for diversity."

John F. Kennedy

Let's Get Started

"The dream doesn't lie in victimization or blame; it lies in hard work, determination and a good education."

Alphonso Jackson

Developing and maintaining an inclusive and diverse workplace is not just about complying with the legislative and organizational code of conduct requirements. What's just as important is that everyone in the workplace displays respectful behavior, which is inclusive and reflects the values of fairness and equal opportunity for all.

Everyone has the right to work in an environment that is safe, respectful and free from harassment, where it's easy to do the best job possible.

This Learning Short-take® will develop your skills in balancing the application of relevant legislation and Code of Conduct policies in the workplace with displaying acceptable workplace behaviors of respect, fairness and transparency in all interactions.

INCLUSION AND DIVERSITY

Part 1

Inclusion and Diversity

"I think there's just one kind of folks - Folks."

Harper Lee,
To Kill a Mockingbird

Diversity in the workplace is quickly becoming recognized as a low cost, high return value for corporations and small businesses. More than just a diversity policy, a commitment to work place diversity helps businesses create a safe and meaningful environment in which people thrive.

By embracing diversity in the workplace companies demonstrate to their employees that they are seen, recognized and valued; a workplace that is inclusive of human characteristics such as race, spirituality, gender, sexual orientation or status as a disabled person. Essentially, companies that harness workplace diversity allow their business to attract and retain quality staff. This translates into the willingness of employees to expend greater effort, apply greater creativity in their jobs and therefore increase productivity.

What is an Inclusive and Diverse Workplace?

Workforce Diversity

The term workforce diversity refers to "the mix" of employees within a workplace. Age, race, marital status, sexual orientation, disability and religion are some of the contributing factors to a diverse workplace. An organization that embraces a diverse workforce policy means being open and inclusive and can draw on and access the best possible pool of available talent.

Diverse and Inclusive Workplace

A diverse and inclusive workplace is a workplace in which every employee is treated equally, and with fairness and respect. It is a workplace where decisions about recruitment, promotion, salary and training opportunities are made based on fairness and with equal opportunity for all.

The Challenge

The challenge for organizations, leaders, managers and employees is to build a diverse and inclusive workplace that goes beyond the words in a diversity policy statement. It is a workplace where equality, fairness and respect is the norm and at all times ensures that there is zero tolerance and swift action on behaviors that are unacceptable.

Complete Activity # 1
Initial Skills Assessment

Activity 1: Initial Skills Assessment

Understanding the importance of a diverse and inclusive workplace and knowing your role in contributing to it is critical to personal and organizational success. This assessment covers the key skills in understanding and contributing to a diverse and inclusive workplace in order to improve work performance for all.

1. Rate yourself on each of the techniques.

7 is competent and confident, little need for improvement
4 is average, needs improvement
1 is uncomfortable, major need for improvement

2. Also - write your reasoning for your answer.

- Note specific areas of improvement related to each diversity and inclusion skill that you would like to develop. Be sure to include your reasons for your rating in each skill, as this reasoning will be a key part of the initial goal setting session with your coach.
- Start thinking about a personal development plan and identify two things you could do to improve your skills in this area and write them in the space provided.

I..	Rating	Reasoning
Consciously strive for a workplace that is diverse and inclusive free from harassment and discrimination.	1 2 3 4 5 6 7	
Understand and practice appropriate workplace conduct and comply with company policy for personal and professional behavior at work.	1 2 3 4 5 6 7	
Treat all of my work colleagues with the same level of respect and fairness regardless of their personal background or differences.	1 2 3 4 5 6 7	
Take appropriate action when I see examples of inappropriate workplace behavior.	1 2 3 4 5 6 7	

Activity 1: Continued

I..	Rating	Reasoning
Understand the impact of Equal Employment Opportunity (EEO) and Anti-Discrimination Legislation on my workplace.	1 2 3 4 5 6 7	
Can explain what constitutes sexual harassment in the workplace and what 'does not' constitute sexual harassment.	1 2 3 4 5 6 7	
Can define workplace bullying and provide behavioral examples.	1 2 3 4 5 6 7	
Know the policy for grievance or complaint handling within my organization and understand my responsibilities in the process.	1 2 3 4 5 6 7	
I am transparent and fair when making decisions about recruitment, promotions or pay increases.	1 2 3 4 5 6 7	

Personal development plan ideas:

1

2

Now update your Learning Journal (page 79)

The Business Case for Diversity and Inclusion

Equal Opportunity legislation and discrimination, harassment, bullying and victimization laws are in place to compel employers and all employees to strive for a workplace that is diverse and inclusive for all.

Ensuring that everyone complies with legal requirements and displays acceptable behavior in the workplace benefits everyone.

> "Small is the number of people who see with their eyes and think with their minds."
>
> Albert Einstein

Benefits of Diversity and Inclusion to the Business

- Maximizes productivity by selecting the best person for the job from the widest available candidate pool.

- Ensures robust business growth and organizational sustainability due to the more open candidate selection criteria where the most suitable people get promoted.

- Reduces training costs where the appropriate people are being trained in the appropriate things.

- Minimizes staff turnover and savings on internal and external recruitment costs: employees see fairness and transparency in the HR process.
- Reduces the loss of intellectual capital when valued staff leave.
- Reduces litigation costs and limits negative publicity through a clearly articulated corporate diversity policy and all 'walking the talk'.

Benefits of Diversity and Inclusion to the Employee

- All employees are able to work productively in a non-threatening environment.
- All employees know the process for promotion or salary increases is fair and transparent and not based on rewarding inappropriate behavior.
- All employees are equally developed to their potential.

"People are pretty much alike. Its only that our differences are more susceptible to definition than our similarities."

Linda Ellerbee

The Risks

"Prejudices subsist in people's imagination long after they have been destroyed by their experience."

Ernest Dimnet

There are a number of risks to employers and employees if every effort is not made to build and maintain a diverse and inclusive workplace. Much media emphasis has been placed on legal risk and related legal costs however it's a more complex issue. Damage to an organization's or individual's reputation, the impact of unacceptable behavior in the wider organizational context and the emotional damage to affected employees cannot be under-estimated.

Legal Risk

Non-compliance with legislation applying to discrimination, harassment, bullying and victimization is punishable by law. Both organizations and individual employees may be liable under legislation with large monetary penalties and criminal charges possible. Refer to the relevant legislation in your organization or region for specific information.

Financial Risk

The financial cost of non-compliance with legislation is significant and can be the responsibility of both the organization and individual employees. In addition to litigation and damages there is the cost of decreased productivity. Fines can also be incurred under Occupational Health and Safety laws.

Reputational Risk

Research has shown that so called "hygiene factors" such as flexible working practices, organizational culture and reputation are significant factors when a potential employee considers joining an organization. Just one poorly handled workplace incident can quickly slur the organization's a reputation with the perception that it promotes a culture that excludes a particular group or does not embrace diversity. Even if the reputation is inaccurate or outdated the perception can be difficult and costly to change.

Complete Activity # 2
Benefits and Risks in a Diverse and Inclusive Workplace

Activity 2: Benefits and Risks in a Diverse and Inclusive Workplace

1

A) List three **benefits to the organization** of developing and maintaining a diverse and inclusive workplace.

1. _____

2. _____

3. _____

B) Relative to your workplace, list two **benefits to you** of having a diverse and inclusive workplace.

For example: When I apply for a new role I know my application will be considered equally to others regardless of my background and I know that others will respect my religious beliefs, even though they may be different to others.

1. _____

2. _____

Activity 2: Continued

C) In the left hand column of the table below, complete the three words beginning with L, F, and R to state the three areas of risk. Then, complete the table with an **example of each risk to you and the organization** if a diverse and inclusive workplace is not built and maintained.

	Risk to Me (as an Employee)	Risk to the Organization
L _____ Risk		
F _____ Risk		
R _____ Risk		

Activity 2 - Check your Answers

A) List three **benefits to the organization** of developing and maintaining a diverse and inclusive workplace.

If you wrote any three of the following, you are correct
- Maximizes productivity by selecting the best person for the job from the widest available candidate pool.
- Ensures a robust business growth and organizational sustainability due to the more open candidate selection criteria where the most suitable people get promoted.
- Reduces training costs where the appropriate people are being trained in the appropriate things.
- Minimizes staff turnover and savings on internal and external recruitment costs: employees see fairness and transparency in the HR process.
- Reduces the loss of intellectual capital when valued staff leave.
- Reduces litigation costs and limits negative publicity through a clearly articulated corporate diversity policy and all 'walking the talk'.

B) Relative to your workplace, list two **benefits to you** of having a diverse and inclusive workplace.

For example: When I apply for a new role I know my application will be considered equally to others regardless of my background and I know that others will respect my religious beliefs, even though they may be different to others.

If you wrote two of the following, you are correct
- I am able to work productively in a non-threatening environment.
- I know the process for promotion or salary increases is fair and transparent and not based on rewarding inappropriate behavior.
- I am being developed to my potential equally.

C) In the left hand column of the table below, complete the three words beginning with L, F, and R to state the three areas of risk. Then, complete the table with an **example of each risk to you and the organization** if a diverse and inclusive workplace is not built and maintained.

	Risk to Me (as an Employee)	**Risk to the Organization**
Legal Risk	Legal action being taken against me personally. My actions causing legal costs for the organization.	Legal action being taken against the organization. Public records showing legal cases against the organization.
Financial Risk	Possible job loss, potential personal costs in legal fees.	High Legal costs. Potential loss of business due to media coverage and negative customer perception. Higher marketing costs to recover from reputational damage.
Reputational Risk	Damage to my reputation, performance, emotional trauma, loss of relationships, lack of promotion and possible job loss.	Negative media coverage and negative customer perception. Brand value damaged.

Now update your Learning Journal (page 79)

Implementing Diversity

There are multiple dimensions of diversity, which include race or ethnicity, gender, sexual orientation, culture, religion, age or ability. Any of those, and even intersections of those dimensions of diversity, may be found to have an impact on the overall performance in an organization.

Transformation from Diversity Compliance to Diversity Commitment

Many organizations discover when they embark on the transformation journey that changes do take place, which support organizational goals far beyond meeting legislative requirements. These include building a more respectful inclusive work environment and a move from diversity compliance to diversity commitment.

> "If your lens is prejudice, you're wearing the wrong prescription."
>
> Carrie Latet

An organization committed to this transformation in organizational culture, where every employee is engaged and contributes to their full potential, that is, from 'exclusive' to 'inclusive', is able to support organizational goals, maximize employee retention and subsequently lift customer satisfaction and productivity.

Communicating a consistent and engaging message can support buy-in and enhance both actual organizational value and the impact of a diversity policy.

1

"Diversity isn't an idea. It's a competitive weapon."

Raymond W. Smith,
Chairman & CEO, Bell Atlantic

Leader and Employee Knowledge and Awareness

Knowledge and awareness are the cornerstones on which a respectful and inclusive workplace can be built by Leaders and Employees.

- Leaders as well as Managers need to 'walk the talk', effectively cascading diversity and inclusive values down through an organization.

  An inclusive leadership approach values and leverages diversity among its employees and recognizes the importance of human capital and employee engagement to the organization's success.

- Employees also have a major role to play in gaining insight into their own attitude to diversity in terms of culture, values, beliefs, biases, both in an historical context and the impact they have on other individual's.

LOCATING POLICIES AND LEGISLATION

Part 2

Locating Policies and Legislation

1

Unacceptable workplace behavior is behavior that treats an individual or group of people less favorably than others and does not reflect the key values of respect, fairness and transparency.

It is important to recognize that workplace employment law differs by country or local jurisdiction. While policies and procedures may be locally based and designed to meet local conditions, the overarching terms, definitions and examples apply to all employees. Grounds for discrimination may vary depending on your location.

This part of the Learning Short-take® is designed for you to know the exact terminology, definitions and your rights and responsibilities. You may have received this information from your employer when joining the organization or in communication updates, or it may be available to you on the company website. General information for your country or jurisdiction may be found on public service websites. The benefit of gathering this information now, is that you can refer to throughout the rest of this Learning Short-take® and in the future.

Complete Activity # 3a
Organizational Definition Search

Complete Activity # 3b
Regional Definition Search

Activity 3a: Organizational Definition Search

It's important to know the exact definition that applies to your organization.

1. Organizational Definition Search

   a. Search your company's intranet or website to locate the legislative definitions and legal requirements for unacceptable workplace behaviors. Information may also be sourced from your HR Department, your organization's diversity policy, induction training kit, or other employee communications.

   b. Does your organization have a Diversity Policy? If so, read it and highlight key points. (If your organization does not have a Diversity Policy, please skip this step and continue with this activity.)

   c. From your search, record the specific behavioral definitions in the table on the following page, together with the source of the information. Also, record key points that are specific to your organization (for example: different policies for age discrimination, racial discrimination, human rights, religion or belief discrimination and so on).

Activity 3a: Continued

1 **Organizational Definition**

Information Source:

Behavior	Definition	Key Points
Discrimination		
Workplace Harassment		
Sexual Harassment		
Bullying		
Victimization		

Now update your Learning Journal (page 79)

Activity 3b: Regional Definition Search

1. Now that you have determined how your organization defines these terms, compare this with how they are defined by your Country, State or specific jurisdiction.

2. City/State/Country Definition Search.

   a. Search the Internet or locate the legislative definitions and legal requirements for unacceptable workplace behaviors.

   Some examples of websites* to assist you in your search are:

United States Of America	www.eeoc.gov.com
Canada	www.chrc.ccdp.ca
United Kingdom	www.direct.gov.uk
Australia	www.hreoc.gov.au
New Zealand	www.hrc.co.nz
Hong Kong	www.eoc.org.hk

   *These websites are correct at the time of publishing.

Activity 3b: Continued

1 b. Record the specific definition in the table below, together with the source of the information. Legislation can also vary from State to State within a Country so double check your information.

Regional Definition

Information Source:

Behavior	Definition
Discrimination	
Workplace Harassment	
Sexual Harassment	
Bullying	
Victimization	

c. Save the website details as a favorite so you can refer to it later. Print relevant pages and keep this information with this Learning Short-take® for future reference.

Important Note: For the remainder of this Learning Short-take®, make sure that the information you use in completing case studies and activities is applicable for your location and organization.

Now update your Learning Journal (page 79)

WORKPLACE DISCRIMINATION

Part 3

tpc

Workplace Discrimination

Note: So that the definitions and examples within this Learning Short-take® are relevant to you, refer to the previous activity for specific definitions for your organization and location. When examining grounds for discrimination, definitions can vary widely from country to country and also within states and jurisdictions within the same country. If in doubt, seek the advice of your HR Department or seek professional legal advice.

Workplace Discrimination Defined

All employees have the right to be treated fairly in the workplace. Workplace discrimination refers to discriminatory employment practices where some employees are treated less favorably than others based on for example their gender, religion or creed, pregnancy, political affiliation, language abilities, citizenship, disability, or sexual orientation, marital status, military veteran status or age.

Human Rights legislation provides the foundation stone of the discrimination laws in most countries, and it's interesting to see how recent some of the inclusions in these laws are. Grounds for discrimination are constantly under review and are being updated, therefore it is an advantage for all employees to keep up to date.

There are two types of workplace discrimination: direct and indirect.

Direct Discrimination

Direct Discrimination is less than favorable treatment in employment or the provision of goods and services, on the grounds of (including but not limited to) gender, pregnancy, homosexuality or transgender, criminal record, race, disability, age, marital status, and carers' responsibilities.

Potential issues in employment include recruitment and selection practices, promotion/career-planning activities, and termination of employment (including resignation and redundancy).

Behavioral Responsibilities

- Employers should not make recruitment, promotion, training or termination decisions based on factors that are not relevant to an individual's ability to perform a particular job, that is, on a person's race, sex, age sexual preference, medical history, disability and so on.
- Individuals should not treat their fellow employees, customers, managers and others less favorably because of these reasons.

What does Direct Discrimination look like in the workplace? Examples:

- Deciding not to employ women with children believing 'they won't be committed to the job' because they will need to look after their children.
- Discounting a potential applicant because they are 'too old' when age has nothing to do with their ability to carry out the job.
- Discounting a staff member's application for promotion because you know they have suffered from a mental illness.
- Not promoting someone to a senior executive position due to his or her sexual preference.

Indirect Discrimination

Indirect Discrimination is less than favorable treatment on the grounds of a condition, requirement or practice, which may disadvantage others due to being of the same sex, different race, have a disability, be of a specific age or of an alternative religion.

Behavioral Responsibilities

- Employers should not impose employment practices or requirements that are not critical to normal business operations.
- Employers should consider whether a requirement/condition might have a disproportionate impact on a particular group of employees before imposing that requirement/condition.

What does Indirect Discrimination look like in the workplace? Examples:

- A requirement to be over a certain height (for example 6' or 183cm) could indirectly discriminate against women and some ethnic groups.
- A requirement to work on some religious days could indirectly discriminate against some religions.

Complete Activity # 4
Discrimination Case Study

Activity 4: Discrimination Case Study

Read the following case study and answer the questions below. There is no one correct answer. You may also like to do research using your organization's or country's website sources from Activity 3.

Sally attended an employment interview and later the same day was offered the job over the phone. She accepted the position and two days later received written confirmation of the employment offer. A day later, Sally obtained a second letter stating that the offer of employment had been withdrawn. She was informed that her former manager, Tom, had advised her new employer that Sally had previously suffered from a psychiatric condition and had been hospitalized for a suicide attempt during her employment. He did not indicate whether her condition impacted on Sally's performance in the position.

Her new employer claimed that a person with Sally's condition could pose occupational health and safety risks not only to herself but also to clients and other employees in the workplace.

Sally stated that her impairment (panic/anxiety attacks) was diagnosed 12 months before the job interview and that she was not required to disclose the condition, as it did not affect her ability to do the job.

1. Explain why this is a **Direct Discrimination** case.

2. What are the key issues in the case?

Activity 4: Continued

1

3. How could the new employer have more effectively handled this situation?

4. Given your knowledge of the legislation relevant to your region and your company's policy on this issue what could be the implications of any claim Sally might make:

- For management

- For the organization

Now update your Learning Journal (page 79)

tpc

WORKPLACE HARASSMENT

Part 4

Workplace Harassment

1 Most employees, who are aware of their rights regarding harassment of a sexual or bullying nature, are glad to have the safety net of legislation and company policies and find it comes naturally to display respect, and fairness in their dealings with others. However, some employees say that workplace harassment legislation and accompanying company policy is restrictive. In their view legislation has removed the fun and playfulness from the workplace and made it too serious.

Unfortunately, the fun for this minority is usually at someone else's expense. What is unacceptable for anyone is the experience of being uncomfortable at work, offended, intimidated or physically or mentally affected by inappropriate behavior. Harassment and bullying are no joking matter.

In defining what constitutes harassment and bullying, it is the seen and unseen impact of the behavior on the affected individual NOT the intent of the individual carrying out the act which is considered under law. "I didn't mean it" or "they are overreacting" is in most cases not a sufficient reason to explain away inappropriate behavior.

Of all workplace behaviors, harassment seems to be the one that is made worse by a "group mentality". Individuals who would usually not behave in an inappropriate manner get caught up in "group think" and are sometimes so intimidated by the bullying or harassing individual that they are too scared to speak up or stop the inappropriate behavior.

Work functions, holiday parties and social events where alcohol is involved and everyone appears to relax are often the source of serious harassment claims. Such functions are still deemed to be work events and all employees and managers have the same duty of care at such functions as in the normal workplace.

Sexual Harassment

Sexual Harassment is:

- Any "unwelcome" conduct of a "sexual nature", that would be considered offensive, humiliating or intimidating to a reasonable person.
- Normally an ongoing series of events, however legally, just one act can constitute harassment.

Types of Sexual Harassment:

- Includes "quid pro quo" where there is the promise of some benefit (if accepted) or the threat of detriment (if denied). For example: a person with authority over another worker demands sexual favors in exchange for a work-related benefit or who carries through on a threat because his or her request for sexual favors was rejected.
- Also includes a hostile work environment where the workplace is "sexually permeated". For Example: Posters of naked people, lewd jokes, offensive emails, indecent exposure, leering and so on.

"What lies behind us and what lies before us are tiny matters, compared to what lies within us."

Ralph Waldo Emerson

Sexual Harassment is not:

- A relationship or behavior that is freely accepted by everyone involved. Such friendships, sexual or otherwise, are a private matter.
- It's commonplace in many workplaces that relationships develop. Over one third of romances are reported to have started in the workplace. However, everyone needs to be aware of the differences between harassment and a behavior that is accepted by and consented to by both parties.

What does Sexual Harassment look like in the workplace? Examples:

Individuals should not:

- Touch co-workers.
- Distribute jokes or photos through company email or other means of a sexually explicit nature.
- Ask co-workers about their sexual experiences or sexual preference.
- Discuss sexual issues in the workplace or at work functions.
- Repeatedly ask another co-worker out on a date.

Complete Activity # 5
Sexual Harassment Case Study

Activity 5: Sexual Harassment Case Study

Read the following case study and answer the questions below. There is no one correct answer. You may also like to do research using your organization's or country's website sources from the previous activity.

Sue recently began work for a new employer. Early into her employment she was approached by a co-worker, Nick, and asked her out on a date. Sue politely declined the invitation and indicated that she was already in a long-term relationship. Shortly after, at the company's Annual Celebration party, a very drunken Nick approached her again. He touched her on the breast and made a lurid suggestion for sex, which offended Sue greatly. Sue demanded an immediate apology. Nick refused to apologize and said that Sue had led him on.

Sue lodged a complaint with her manager Tom, who addressed the situation by transferring Sue to another work site (claiming that she had made several errors in her work in her previous position). During her first day at the new work site, her new co-workers subjected Sue to belittling and humiliating comments and behavior. Management encouraged and supported these comments. It was obvious that everyone knew about the complaint and why Sue had been transferred.

Sue left the work site and has not returned. She has sought legal advice and is currently pursuing her claim through the relevant authorities.

1. What are the relevant issues in this case?

2. How could the employer have more effectively handled this situation?

Activity 5: Continued

3. Given your knowledge of the legislation relevant to your region and your company's policy on this issue what might be the outcome of any claim Sue might make:

   a. Through her organization

   b. Through an external party such as a court

Now update your Learning Journal (page 79)

Bullying

Bullying can happen to children in the schoolyard, or adults in the workplace. Bullying can manifest itself in the physical sense or via what is becoming more apparent, cyber-bullying using cell phones, the Internet or other forms of social media such as social networking sites and blogs.

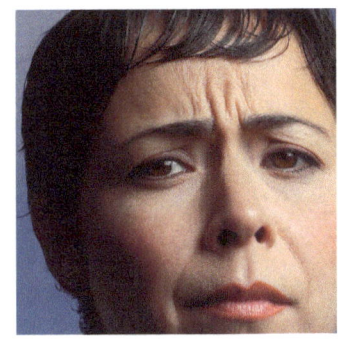

Definition of Workplace Bullying

A bully is defined as someone who is "a person who uses strength or power to oppress, coerce or persecute others by fear" (Concise Oxford Dictionary).

"… all those repeated actions and practices that are directed to one or more workers, which are unwanted by the victim, which may be done deliberately or unconsciously, … cause humiliation, offense, and distress, and that may interfere with job performance and/or cause an unpleasant working environment." Einarsen, 1999

Important components of Einarsen's definition are: Repeated, Unwanted, Causes Harm and Interferes with Work.

1

What is Bullying?

Bullying is also commonly referred to as mobbing, harassment, abuse, incivility, and psychological aggression, being a victim, target, or working in a hostile work environment.

Bullying is the repeated and deliberate abuse of another person. With the exception of group bullying the majority of bullying occurs in private, one on one.

Bullying can occur wherever there is a hierarchal division of power, even just a perception of power, or where there may be differences between individuals for any reason.

However, bullying is not limited to individuals. Corporations, authority figures and governments have used bullying tactics to intimidate others. The common thread of bullying is people abusing power over others although where power is shared it is difficult for individuals to use bullying behaviors to gain power over others.

Bullying in the workplace can include initiation ceremonies, pranks, unfair and excessive criticism, consistently unrealistic work targets, and undervaluing efforts at work. Through awareness, knowledge and commitment bullying behaviors can be prevented and cooperative inclusive behaviors be embraced.

Scope of the Bullying Problem

For individuals the effects can be long lasting and lead to mental health issues, relationship or marital breakdown and a total loss of self worth. Commonly reported effects included stress, social isolation, loss of confidence, headaches, stomach cramps and depression.

For organizations, the consequences of bullying may result in poor work quality, loss of productivity, financial liability and an increase in employee turnover, absenteeism and legal action.

2006 British Survey

Workplace bullying is widespread, according to findings from a British survey in 2006 by the Chartered Institute of Personnel and Development (CIPD) in association with MORI and Kingston Business School. The survey results reported:

- 20% of all UK employees have experienced some form of bullying or harassment over the last two years.
- Groups most likely to become victims of bullying and harassment are black and Asian employees, women and people with a disability.
- Nearly one third (29%) of Asian employees or those from other ethnic groups report having experienced some form of bullying or harassment, compared with 18% of white employees.
- Employees with disabilities are at least twice as likely to report having experienced one or more forms of bullying and harassment (37%), compared with non-disabled employees (18%).

> "If there is to be any peace it will come through being, not having."
>
> Henry Miller

2007 USA Survey

The Workplace Bullying Institute U.S. Workplace Bullying Survey September, 2007 conducted 7,740 online interviews of a panel that is representative of the adult population of the U.S. This is the largest national scientific survey of the phenomenon in the U.S. to date. The key findings of the survey were:

1. Workplace bullying is an epidemic

37% of American workers, an estimated 54 million people, have been bullied at work. It affects half (49%) of American workers, 71.5 million workers, when witnesses are included.

2. Workplace bullying is rife

Bullying is 4 times more prevalent than other forms of "harassment."

3. American employers can and do ignore bullying

In 62% of the cases, when made aware of bullying, employers worsen the problem or simply do nothing, despite losing an estimated 21-28 million workers because of bullying.

4. Most bullies are bosses - the stereotype is real

- 72% of bullies are bosses.
- 55% of those bullied are rank-and-file workers.

5. Bullying most strongly affects women

Bullies target women more frequently (in 57% of cases), especially by other women (in 71% of cases).

6. Bullying is a public health hazard

For 45% of bullied targets, stress affects their health. 33% suffer for more than one year.

7. Bullied individuals are not "crazy", - many fail to even complain

Only 3% of bullied targets file lawsuits. 40% never complain.

8. Perpetrators suffer little despite inflicting suffering

Targets have to stop the vast majority of bullying (77%) by losing their jobs despite being the ones harmed.

"We have become not a melting pot but a beautiful mosaic. Different people, different beliefs, different yearnings, different hopes, different dreams."

Jimmy Carter

2008 Australian Survey

An Australian survey in 2008 of 1,782 respondents, conducted by LinkMe, reported that:

- 41% of respondents said Cyber bullying comes directly from management and bosses.

- Almost half of the respondents said when seeking support and assistance their employers did not take them seriously.

- When let down by their employers, 52.9% of employees are simply left to struggle in an extremely distressing situation with no possibility of resolution whatsoever, according to the survey.

What does Bullying look like in the Workplace? Examples:

Bullying behavior may be directed upwards or downwards and towards co-workers. There is no finite list of bullying behaviors, however, the following types of behavior, where repeated or occurring as part of a pattern of behavior, could be considered bullying:

- Subjecting co-workers to "initiation ceremonies".
- Continuously criticizing co-workers or call them derogatory names.
- Undertaking actions that risk the heath and/or safety of co-workers.
- Playing workplace "pranks" on co-workers.

- Making threats to professional status: Constant criticism, damaging rumors, belittling opinions, undermining authority, assigning meaningless tasks, excluding / ignoring views, public professional humiliation, accusations regarding lack of effort, and unreasonable or inappropriate monitoring.
- Making threats to personal standing: Intimidating, insulting and name calling, criticizing in front of others, questioning judgment and spreading untrue rumors and gossip.
- Creating social isolation: Physical or social isolation, withholding information, preventing access to opportunities.
- Creating obstructionism: Causing others to delay actions, interfering with/blocking work, refusing to provide resources and support.
- Being subjected to constant ridicule and being put down in front of colleagues.
- Being the victim of loud and abusive, threatening or derogatory language usually when other employees are present.
- Leaving offensive messages on email or by telephone, including offensive messages through the use of SMS and material posted on the Internet.

"We need every human gift and cannot afford to neglect any gift because of artificial barriers such as sex or race or class or national origin."

Margaret Mead

Legitimate Authority vs. Bullying

It is important to differentiate between a person's legitimate authority at work, and bullying. All employers have a legal right to direct and control how work is done, and managers have a responsibility to monitor workflow and give feedback and manage performance. Bullying is not legitimate authority.

"Organizations allowing workplace bullying effectively engage in a process of adverse selection in which the best and brightest may be let go at the expense of the most aggressive and uncivil."

Glendinning, 2001

Bullying: A Case Study

When Madhu joined a television production organization, little did she know she would be threatened because she was more capable than her colleagues. Her creativity and innovation made her immediate bosses and colleagues gang up against her "to teach her a lesson". Promotions and pay increases were based on seniority and tenure so management saw little sense in rewarding innovation or working beyond what was absolutely essential. continued >

Coming from a completely different background, having studied in the best schools, graduating from one of India's premier colleges, and belonging to a family of senior bureaucrats, made Madhu think differently to her new colleagues. She had independently decided to follow her career in television production in a foreign country. Her guiding force was not money but passion and belief in what she was doing. Her work was initially plagiarized, stolen and copied. When she reported these issues on moral grounds, individual bullies singled her out by making disparaging remarks, hinting at an affair with a junior, and telling lewd stories about her. When this too did not work, they lobbied to get her transferred and made threatening phone calls at her home. When she reported these incidents to her immediate manager and HR manager no action was taken. When unable to take any further abuse she resigned. The bullying then stopped.

Often in workplace bullying, there is the combination of pressure bullying and corporate bullying. In Madhu's case, it started off with individual bullying going on to include vicarious bullying (two parties engaging in adversarial conflict) and then to serial bullying (persistent bullying which went on for some time, involving inter-departmental teams), culminating in a situation where she felt the only option was to resign. Madhu had documented the incidents in detail and had grounds for legal action against both the individuals involved and the organization.

Complete Activity # 6
Bullying Case Study

Activity 6: Bullying Case Study

1 Read the following case study and answer the questions below. There is no one correct answer. You may also like to do research using your organization's or country's website sources from the previous activity.

During his first week of employment Dave complained that a group of his co-workers cornered him on a building site, exposed themselves to him, then held him while a piece of splintered timber was run up between his legs to his groin. When he objected, his co-workers began calling him obscene names and threatened to take the prank further if he didn't keep quiet.

Dave noticed that several of the other new apprentices had been also subjected to the same treatment and that recently two of them had resigned.

When Dave advised his foreman, Pirro, of the situation, he was told to ignore the behavior and to "lighten up". Dave was told by Pirro "that all new apprentices go through it in the first couple of weeks ", "I went through it twenty years ago it's the way we do things round here".

Dave was so traumatized by the experience; he resigned and has not sought a job in the building industry since.

1. What are the relevant issues in this case?

___

2. How could the employer have more effectively handled this situation?

___

Activity 6: Continued

3. Given your knowledge of the legislation relevant to your region and your company's policy on this issue what could be the implications of any claim Dave might make:

a. For management

b. For the organization

Now update your Learning Journal (page 79)

1

Cyber bullying (also referred to as e-Bullying)

The rise of technology in the workplace has another unfortunate side effect: the potential for threatening behavior between individuals. This 'Cyber bullying' is something employers increasingly need to be concerned with and should bring their policies and procedures up to date. This should result in fewer complaints and where incidents do occur, the ability to resolve them early before they significantly impact employee productivity.

Cyber bullying is a form of bullying that is carried out through SMS or an Internet service such as email, chat room, blog, discussion group or other forms of instant messaging.

With mobile technology and the Internet, it's much easier and less constraining for the bully. They don't have to look at the other person and the technology is instant.

Cyber bullying has long been more closely associated with the intentional bullying of children and teenagers through SMS and online by their peers. However adults and the workplace are not immune from Cyber bullying.

Although Cyber bullying is a relatively new mechanism of bullying, the power relationships remain the same.

Examples of Cyber bullying

A range of different examples of bullying at work using electronic means may include:

Offensive e-mail. Sending offensive e-mail to a colleague even if it's supposed to be a joke in which a person might be offended by the content of the message or any photographs that are attached. Continuing to send similar messages, having been asked to stop, constitutes bullying.

E-mail threats also include relatively inoffensive messages in terms of content but the implied meaning behind the message can constitute a form of bullying. An example of this might be where a superior is bombarding an employee with far more work than they can handle while other members of the team are not being treated in the same way.

Sharing A Person's Private Data Online. Cyber bullying can take on a much more sinister meaning when people post personal details which are then available to the general public and which wouldn't normally be shared with complete strangers. This can include posting home addresses and phone numbers for all to see.

Cyber bullying SMS/Text Messages. It doesn't need to be e-mail at work. Any threats or offensive comments made about somebody to their mobile/cell phone is a very real form of Cyber bullying, even if the sender didn't intend to harm the person.

1

> "Prejudice is the child of ignorance."
>
> William Hazlitt

E-malice

E-mail is by far the most common method of Cyber bullying at work. It is the predominant form of business communication and the channel of choice in today's workplace.

Experts on bullying believe that many bullies can lack good communication skills and therefore the impersonal nature of email makes an ideal tool for them to victimize others.

It took a while for people to recognize that sending an unpleasant e-mail and copying in a number of people who didn't need to be involved in the email exchange was a form of bullying. Given that tribunals and courts are increasingly ordering the disclosure of e-mails, employees should think twice before writing a contemptible or adverse e-mail they would not be able to easily explain.

The test is, would you actually say to someone's face what you're putting in the e-mail or where the content of the e-mail may be sensitive? If you are unsure, perhaps save it as a draft and go back to it a couple of hours later to read it again, before sending it.

What to do about e-malice

Unfortunately it is not immediately possible to check where an email has come from. You have to trust that the named writer is genuine, but it is not always wise to make this assumption.

The best practice is

- If a name is not familiar, it may be safer not to open the email.
- If the sender is a known bully, or if they have sent unpleasant or annoying messages before, then record the incident, and save it in a separate file.
- If the bullying happens through a personal email account, report it to the sender's email account provider. You can find this address after the @ sign.
- If it is not obvious who the sender is and there is continual bullying using email, then there are methods to trace senders. Your manager and IT department can assist.
- If it is appropriate to your situation, follow the grievance procedure outlined in Part 6 of this Learning Short-take® - Impact, Prevention and Taking Action.

"[People] may be said to resemble not the bricks of which a house is built, but the pieces of a picture puzzle, each differing in shape, but matching the rest, and thus bringing out the picture."

Felix Adler

"We need diversity of thought in the world to face the new challenges."

Tim Berners-Lee

Social networking

Social networking sites such as Facebook, MySpace, Bebo, and Twitter with their audience of millions perhaps cause the greatest potential for humiliation and stress because of comments directed to specific individuals and also directed to organizations' products and services.

Posting blogs and comments on social networking sites. Quite often a person may not experience any direct form of Cyber bullying but instead the bullies are leaving nasty or offensive comments or photos about them on blogs and social networking sites that can often be viewed by others. This intimidation would also fall under the umbrella of Cyber bullying.

Spreading lies and malicious gossip. Social networking sites, forums and blogs are often the most common ways in which people become harass and victimize other people and is considered Cyber bullying.

Complete Activity # 7
Cyber Bullying Case Study

Activity 7: Cyber Bullying Case Study

Read the following case study and answer the questions below. There is no one correct answer. You may also like to do research using your organization's or country's website sources from Activity 3.

Troy was aware he had a 'secret admirer' at work. He knew it was his colleague Amanda whom he'd had lunch with a few times and socialized together at mutual friends' parties. She wanted to establish a closer friendship or relationship with Troy, and Amanda used e-mail to 'test the waters' first, the fear of rejection she thought would be far less if an approach is made that way. Troy spoke with Amanda immediately on receipt of the first email and wanted to maintain a casual friendship with her but nothing more. The emails continued, each time becoming more explicit. Each time Troy either sent Amanda an email rejecting her advance or spoke personally with her.

Troy's manager Jess assigned a project where Troy and Amanda were on the same project team. Troy spoke with Jess and explained the situation. Jess sympathetically took Troy off the project team. Jess didn't take any further action or report the case.

Over the next six months, Amanda continued to send Troy emails, SMS messages outside working hours, and then Amanda posted personal information about him on the company's Facebook page.

Troy took legal action, and Amanda was prosecuted for harassment due to her persistent e-mails, SMS messages and entries on the social networking site after it was clear that Troy had rejected her.

1. What are the relevant issues in this case?

2. How could the employer have more effectively handled this situation?

Activity 7: Continued

1

3. Given your knowledge of the legislation relevant to your region and your company's policy on this issue what could be the implications of any claim Troy might make:

a. For management

b. For the organization

Now update your Learning Journal (page 79)

Victimization

What is Victimization?

Victimization in the workplace is a term used in discrimination law to describe action by an employer or employee against another employee, in retaliation for initiating or supporting complaint proceedings. Examples may include:

- Made a complaint about discrimination directly to the person or organization who treated them unfairly.
- Sent a complaint about discrimination to an Anti-Discrimination Authority.
- Before or after giving evidence against the employer at a tribunal.
- Gave advice or information about discrimination to someone else.
- Acted as a witness for someone who has been discriminated against.
- Refusal to promote an employee because he or she had invoked a grievance procedure.

Victimization can even take place after employment has finished, for example, when an employer refuses to give a former employee, who had begun tribunal proceedings, a reference. People who have experienced discrimination, harassment or victimization are often afraid to speak out about what has happened, for fear that it will make the situation worse.

Victimization is unlawful because it tries to punish people for speaking out about discrimination and harassment, or tries to stop people from continuing with a complaint. Any law against victimization is there to encourage people to speak out against discrimination and harassment, by protecting them when they make a complaint.

What can be done about it?

- If you are victimized, you can speak out and ask for the behavior to stop.
- If this is difficult to do you might ask another person, such as a friend or fellow worker, to speak out for you.
- If you are able to, you may wish to talk to your supervisor or manager about your concern.
- You could seek help from an Advocacy Service, or a representative of your Union.
- You can get in touch with an advisor at the Equal Opportunity Authority in your State or Country. An advisor at the Authority can help by answering your questions on victimization telling you about the complaint procedure.

Implications for Employers

Victimization can be generally upheld even when the original complaint is not successful. In cases where a person is alleging discrimination or harassment, employers must ensure that the complainant/witnesses are not subjected to acts or threatened acts of victimization.

Complete Activity # 8
Victimization Situations

Activity 8: Victimization Situations

Read the following case study and answer the questions below. There is no one correct answer. You may also like to do research using your organization's or country's website sources from Activity 3.

1. *Anna was dismissed after lodging a complaint of sexual harassment against a co-worker.*
   Why is this victimization?

2. *Peter's co-worker had been taunting other workers about their sexuality, repeatedly calling them derogatory names. When Peter complained to his boss about the comments, the co-worker then said: "I'm going to get you for this."*
   Why is this victimization?

3. *Marcia saw a boy being told to leave a store for being of different ethnic background. Later, the manager refused to let Marcia back into his store when he found out that she had agreed to be a witness in a complaint of racial discrimination made against him by the boy.*
   Why is this victimization?

Activity 8 - Check your Answers

1. *Anna was dismissed after lodging a complaint of sexual harassment against a co-worker.*

   Why is this victimization?

   Anna was victimized for trying to deal with discrimination internally in her organization.

2. *Peter's co-worker had been taunting other workers about their sexuality, repeatedly calling them derogatory names. When Peter complained to his boss about the comments, the co-worker then said: "I'm going to get you for this."*

   Why is this victimization?

   Peter was victimized for supporting someone with a discrimination matter.

3. *Marcia saw a boy being told to leave a store for being of different ethnic background. Later, the manager refused to let Marcia back into his store when he found out that she had agreed to be a witness in a complaint of racial discrimination made against him by the boy.*

   Why is this victimization?

   Marcia was victimized for supporting someone with a discrimination matter.

Now update your Learning Journal (page 79)

Job Aid - Defining Workplace Behavior

The 'Defining Workplace Behavior' Job Aid is a handy reference card of key terms and definitions.

1

"One day our descendants will think it incredible that we paid so much attention to things like the amount of melanin in our skin or the shape of our eyes or our gender instead of the unique identities of each of us as complex human beings."

Franklin Thomas

THE INCLUSIVE AND DIVERSE WORKPLACE IN ACTION

Part 5

Building a Diverse and Inclusive Workplace

An understanding of what unacceptable behavior is in the workplace is the starting point, but should not be the only focus in your skill development. Building an inclusive and diverse workplace across the organization is the key to managing diversity successfully.

For Leaders

Implementing a diversity policy where all employees are included builds the bottom line through productivity and loyalty. Leaders should also actively disseminate and implement this policy throughout the workplace.
This inclusive leadership approach recognizes the importance of human capital and employee engagement to the organization's success.

For Employees

It is equally important for all employees to develop skills and behaviors that will create a diverse and inclusive workplace. Employees have a major role to play focusing on building awareness about one's own diversity in terms of culture, values, beliefs and biases.

Three key behaviors when building a diverse and inclusive workplace are Respect, Fairness and Transparency.

Respect

The respectful workplace is a place of mutual respect for all employees, where no one feels harassed or scared. The building blocks of a respectful workplace are equality, accepting differences and appreciating differences.

1. **Equality.** We must be willing to acknowledge that all employees have an equal right to work. Each person should have an equal opportunity to make the best use of his or her abilities regardless of race, sex, religion, national origin or any other characteristics.

2. **Accepting Differences.** Acknowledging equality requires the ability to accept differences. We all work with people who are different from us. They may look different, sound different, and even behave differently. They may practice a different religion or come from a different background. Realization that these differences do not prevent us from work is a key foundation stone to respect.

3. **Appreciating Diversity.** Beyond accepting differences is the ability to appreciate the diversity that exists in the workplace. The variety of experiences, viewpoints, attitudes, abilities and ways of thinking is an organizational advantage. This diversity adds depth and strength to the workplace.

Respectful language and thoughts include: "I respect you as an individual and your values", "I may not like you; however I am courteous and can show empathy to your point of view", "I may not agree with you, however I listen to you", "I keep confidences and am discrete with information". It is essential that we examine our behavior and actions to ensure that we are doing our part to promote a respectful workplace.

Fairness

Fairness in the workplace is where all employees are treated without bias and without prejudice regardless of the manager's relationship with them. What is fair? Fairness usually depends on individual perspective. What is fair to one person may be ridiculously unfair in someone else's eyes. However there are components of fairness that should exist in every workplace.

Fairness can be demystified in clear, easy to understand organizational policies and procedures.

Remember, it's not about everyone being best friends in the workplace. Personal friendships often need to be set aside so that individuals remain objective and fair.

Transparency

Transparency in the workplace is an open and honest communication channel between employees and leadership regarding workplace behavior issues, which has a significant positive impact on workplace culture overall.

Everyone needs to know how decisions affecting employees are made; processes need to be clearly articulated and clearly understood by all and adhered to by managers.

Guidelines for Behaving in a Respectful, Fair and Transparent Manner

Guidelines for Everyone

- Think before you speak. Assess the impact of your message on the person you are talking with. Review written communication to ensure messages cannot be misconstrued or offend.
- Use the 'send later', or 'save to draft' button on email but if in doubt DON'T (this applies to telling a joke, sending an email, carrying out a practical joke).
- Show common courtesy; not interrupting, listening to others, calling others by their name, whatever is culturally appropriate courteous behavior. Change your message to meet specific needs.
- When you first join an organization, don't assume you can behave the same way as you have in previous organizations. Observe others behavior, you will soon work out what is acceptable and what isn't. Read the company's policies and attend any available training.
- Challenge organizational policies and practices that may be exclusionary. Stand up and speak out when others are not valued or their ideas or views are not taken into account.

"In overcoming prejudice working together is even more effective than talking together."

Ralph W Sockman

Guidelines for Managers

- Be clear about setting performance expectations and be a role model. Be clear about what's acceptable and what isn't acceptable. Act quickly on any unacceptable behavior and give praise when you see examples of the desired behaviors.

- Help your employees to fully understand both the written and unwritten "rules" of the organization.

- Re-examine how you have traditionally judged the characteristics or qualities you look for in high potential employees. Be fair and demonstrate no favoritism to one staff member or colleague over another.

- Welcome differences in approach and opinion, and create opportunities for everyone to be able to contribute and succeed. Involve diverse groups in solving problems and developing opportunities.

- Broaden your view about diversity and inclusion beyond just race or gender issues. Talk openly about the tension between the need to value and accept others and the desire for shared organizational values.

- Take time to find out about the backgrounds of your staff (in an appropriate manner). Ask about religious holidays, practices and any specific customs that are relevant to the workplace. Be discrete and respect confidentiality around any sensitive issues within your team.

Complete Activity # 9
Respect, Fairness and Transparency

Activity 9: Respect, Fairness and Transparency

Do the following statements describe the behaviors of Respect, Fairness and Transparency?

Place a ✔ to answer Yes or No to each statement.

	YES	NO
I have to be best friends with everyone to show respect to my employees or to colleagues at work.		
Transparency is about telling employees all the gossip about their colleagues and other managers.		
It's showing respect when everyone gets heard in a team meeting.		
The same employees always get to take leave at Christmas or during Holiday times because I know they have small children. That's fair isn't it?		
I think about both the content and the effect on the receiver before distributing a "funny email".		
It's showing respect when I joke with a Muslim co-worker about her headwear. I joke with everyone and she knows that.		
I didn't get the opportunity to work flexibly when my children were small so I don't give the opportunity to my staff either. That's fair isn't it?		
I try to be transparent by being very clear about what skills and abilities are needed to be promoted to supervisor here and list them in the job advertisement.		
I respect the cultural and religious beliefs of my co-workers.		
It is fair that my manager favors one of my co-workers more favorably. After all he is the manager's son.		

Activity 9 - Check your Answers

	YES	NO
I have to be best friends with everyone to show respect to my employees or to colleagues at work.		✔
Transparency is about telling employees all the gossip about their colleagues and other managers.		✔
It's showing respect when everyone gets heard in a team meeting.	✔	
The same employees always get to take leave at Christmas or during Holiday times because I know they have small children. That's fair isn't it?		✔
I think about both the content and the effect on the receiver before distributing a "funny email".	✔	
It's showing respect when I joke with a Muslim co-worker about her headwear. I joke with everyone and she knows that.		✔
I didn't get the opportunity to work flexibly when my children were small so I don't give the opportunity to my staff either. That's fair isn't it?		✔
I try to be transparent by being very clear about what skills and abilities are needed to be promoted to supervisor here and list them in the job advertisement.	✔	
I respect the cultural and religious beliefs of my co-workers.	✔	
It is fair that my manager favors one of my co-workers more favorably. After all he is the manager's son.		✔

Now update your Learning Journal (page 79)

//tpc//

IMPACT, PREVENTION AND TAKING ACTION

Part 6

Impact of Unacceptable Workplace Behavior

"The wave of the future is not the conquest of the world by a single dogmatic creed but the liberation of the diverse energies of free nations and free men."

John F. Kennedy

Impact on Individuals

For individuals whatever the experience, the outcomes are similar, physical and psychological effects are common and may include health issues, a lack of confidence or self-esteem, stress, depression or even nervous disorders. The impact of which may cause time off work, resignation, redundancy or termination, the latter may result in inquiries and in many cases medical and legal costs.

Impact on Organizations

The organization also suffers internally from the impact of bullying and may cause a dysfunctional working environment, low productivity and more commonly a reduction in moral. Externally the organization also suffers through adverse publicity and poor public image in addition to possible costs associated with a failure to meet legislative provisions, civil and or criminal actions and personal injury claims.

Obligation and Prevention

The obligations and methods of prevention seem relatively simple when compared with the impacts, as described above, to both individuals and organizations. Your research activities carried out during this Learning Short-take® into your local and state laws have provided you with relevant local information, however in general employers are obligated under 'duty of care' to protect workers from any form of harassment. This requires an employer to act on and adequately investigate claims of harassment.

A manager or supervisor that ignores or inadequately deals with a complaint leaves not only the organization but also themselves wide open to legal scrutiny. This scrutiny can be avoided or minimized if the employer can demonstrate they took all reasonable steps to prevent the harassment occurring.

"Judgments prevent us from seeing the good that lies beyond appearances."

Wayne W. Dyer

Taking Action against Physical or Verbal Harassment

1

"An eye for an eye makes the whole world blind."

Mahatma Gandhi, Indian political and spiritual leader (1869 - 1948)

If you experience harassment, if appropriate you should first talk to the person concerned, telling them that you find the behavior offensive and indicating you want the behavior to stop. You can do this verbally or in writing. Hopefully the unacceptable behavior will then stop. You should make notes detailing the offensive behavior including the date it happened, how you felt, what you did about it and who else was present or informed.

If the behavior occurs again, or if you do not wish to speak to the person directly, there are a number of actions you can take:

1. Talk with your manager or supervisor. They are responsible for ensuring a diverse and inclusive workplace. You cannot lose your job for reporting harassment.

2. If the problem involves your manager or supervisor, approach another trusted person or if available, a Human Resources professional.

3. If you are a manager and a staff member approaches you about an issue relating to unacceptable behavior try in the first instance to solve the problem. If you don't feel confident in dealing with the problem refer to another manager or Human Resources department. Remember to maintain confidentiality, investigate thoroughly before making a judgment, and support and protect the person who has made the complaint.

4. Most organizations have in place a grievance or complaints handling procedure for dealing with such issues. Familiarize yourself with it.

5. As an employee, if you feel the internal processes have not adequately dealt with your complaint, there are external agencies that can deal with complaints around harassment and discrimination.

In the instance where someone is threatening physical harm or engaging in physical abuse at work, they are violating the law, as well as your employer's policy. You have a right to be safe at work. Report this behavior immediately.

Complete Activity # 10
Grievance Procedure

Activity 10: Grievance Procedure

1. Obtain a copy of the Grievance or Complaint Handling Procedure for your organization. Hint: You may need to search your intranet, ask your manager, ask the Human Resources Manager or get it from another source.

   a. Read the Procedure carefully.

   b. What are the various responsibilities of the following parties?

      - Your Responsibility

      _____
      _____
      _____

      - Your Manager's Responsibility

      _____
      _____
      _____

      - Organization's Responsibility

      _____
      _____
      _____

2. Investigate the government agency website (examples of which you investigated in Activity 3) relevant to your country. Write the step-by-step procedure for lodging a complaint with the relevant external agency.

   _____
   _____
   _____
   _____

Now update your Learning Journal (page 79)

Section 2
LEARNING JOURNAL

The Learning Journal is used throughout the Learning Short-take® process to record your key learnings, hot tips and things to remember.

Update your Learning Journal at anytime throughout the Learning Short-take® process. Ensure you complete your Learning Journal after you finish each activity. Then turn back to the Participant Guide to continue your learning.

Learning Journal

As you work through this Learning Short-take®, make detailed notes on this page of the lessons you have learned and any useful skill areas. For each lesson or refresher point think about how you could further develop this skill. Your coach will want to discuss these with you in your Skill Development Action Planning meeting.

"…that is what learning is.
You suddenly understand something you've understood all your life, but in a new way."

Doris Lessing

"Act as though it were impossible to fail."

Winston Churchill

"The wise do at once what the fool does later."
Baltasar Gracian (1601-58), Spanish Jesuit priest and author.

Learning or Idea	Action to be taken	Result Expected

Learning Journal - continued

Learning or Idea	Action to be taken	Result Expected

"Anyone who stops learning is old, whether at twenty or eighty."
Henry Ford

Learning or Idea	Action to be taken	Result Expected

2

"If we were to wake up some morning and find that everyone was the same race, creed and color, we would find some other causes for prejudice by noon."

George Aiken

Section 3

SKILL DEVELOPMENT ACTION PLAN

Your Skill Development Action Plan is the last Step in the Learning Short-take® process. After you have completed the Participant Guide and all Activities update your Learning Journal then complete this section.

Skill Development Action Plan

This is the most important part of the program - your individual Skill Development Action Plan.

You need to complete this plan before meeting with your manager or prior to on-going coaching. You will discuss it in detail with your manager or coach as he or she will ensure that you have everything you need to complete the tasks and activities.

Once you have completed your **Skill Development Action Plan** schedule a meeting time with your manager or coach to review your plan. Take your participant guide and all other documentation received during the training course to this meeting.

Remember - you have committed to your **Skill Development Action Plan**, and need to make time to complete your tasks!

"The mind, once stretched by a new idea, never regains its original dimensions."

Oliver Wendell Holmes

"Whatever you can do or dream you can - begin it. Boldness has genius, power and magic."

Johann Wolfgang von Goethe

"Imagination is the eye of the soul."
Joseph Joubert (1754-1824)

Task or activity (Be specific)	Measure (this will help you to know you have achieved it)	Date (Be specific)
Reflect on your Learning Journal. Transfer action items that you can apply to your job. Ensure that you include some 'stretch goals' and also a blend of short, medium and long term goals.	Apart from you, who else is needed to assist you in achieving your goal.	Be specific. A general date such as 'Quarter 1', 'August', or 'by end of year' is vague and more likely to result in not achieving your target. Be specific – e.g. 22nd November.

Ideas for discussion with my manager

Ideas

Congratulations!

You've now completed this Learning Short-take®.

Meet with your Manager/Coach to discuss your Assessment (Activity # 8) and your Skill Development Action Plan.

3

"What is tolerance?
It is the consequence of humanity.
We are all formed of frailty and error;
let us pardon reciprocally each other's folly -
that is the first law of nature."

Voltaire

extra

QUICK REFERENCE

This Quick Reference provides you with a summary of key concepts, models and reference material from Learning Short-takes®. We have also included some quotations to ponder.

Use this section as a quick reference to keep your learning active.

Quick Reference

Anti-discrimination work practices

Following Equal Employment Opportunity (EEO) anti-discrimination law helps to ensure that:

- the best person gets the job
- the right people get trained in the right things
- the best people get promoted
- all employees are developed to their full potential
- all employees are able to work productively in a non-threatening environment
- the organization doesn't end up in court fighting costly discrimination or harassment claims

Diverse and Inclusive Workplace

A diverse and inclusive workplace is a workplace in which every employee is treated with equality, fairness and respect. It is a workplace where decisions about recruitment, promotion, salary and training opportunities are made based on fairness and with equal opportunity for all.

Quick Reference

> **Diversity isn't an idea. It's a competitive weapon.**

Raymond W. Smith,
Chairman & CEO, Bell Atlantic

Workplace Discrimination Defined

All employees have the right to be treated fairly in the workplace. Workplace discrimination refers to discriminatory employment practices where some employees are treated less favorably than others based on their gender, religion or creed, pregnancy, political affiliation, language abilities, citizenship, disability, sexual orientation, marital status, military veteran status or age.

Quick Reference

> **An eye for an eye makes the whole world blind.**

Mahatma Gandhi, Indian political and spiritual leader (1869 – 1948)

“ Courage is fire, and bullying is smoke. ”

Benjamin Disraeli
(British Prime Minister and Novelist. 1804-1881)

Quick Reference

Direct Discrimination

Direct Discrimination is less than favorable treatment in employment or the provision of goods and services, on the grounds of (including but not limited to) gender, pregnancy, homosexuality or transgender, criminal record, race, disability, age, marital status, and carers' responsibilities.

Indirect Discrimination

Indirect Discrimination is less than favorable treatment on the grounds of a condition, requirement or practice, which may disadvantage others due to being of the same sex, different race, have a disability, be of a specific age or of an alternative religion.

Quick Reference

> **Preconceived notions are the locks on the door to wisdom.**
>
> Merry Browne

Sexual Harassment is:

- Any "unwelcome" conduct of a "sexual nature", that would be considered offensive, humiliating or intimidating to a reasonable person.

- Normally an ongoing series of events, however legally, just one act can constitute harassment.

Quick Reference

4

> " I think there's just one kind of folks. Folks. "
>
> Harper Lee, To Kill a Mockingbird

> **If your lens is prejudice, you're wearing the wrong prescription.**

Carrie Latet

Quick Reference

> **Small is the number of people who see with their eyes and think with their minds.**
>
> Albert Einstein

Workplace Bullying

" ...all those repeated actions and practices that are directed to one or more workers, which are unwanted by the victim, which may be done deliberately or unconsciously, ... cause humiliation, offense, and distress, and that may interfere with job performance and/or cause an unpleasant working environment. "

Einarsen, 1999

Quick Reference

Cyber bullying

Cyber bullying is a form of bullying that is carried out through SMS or an Internet service such as email, chat room, blog, discussion group or other forms of instant messaging.

> **What lies behind us and what lies before us are tiny matters, compared to what lies within us.**
>
> Ralph Waldo Emerson

Quick Reference

Victimization

Victimization in the workplace is a term used in discrimination law to describe action by an employer or employee against another employee, in retaliation for initiating or supporting complaint proceedings.

> **Prejudices subsist in people's imagination long after they have been destroyed by their experience.**
>
> Ernest Dimnet

Quick Reference

Key Behaviors of a Diverse and Inclusive Workplace

Respect

The respectful workplace is a place of mutual respect for all employees, where no one feels harassed or scared. The building blocks of a respectful workplace are equality, accepting differences and appreciating differences.

Fairness

Fairness in the workplace is where all employees are treated without bias and without prejudice regardless of the manager's relationship with them.

Transparency

Transparency in the workplace is an open and honest communication channel between employees and leadership regarding workplace behavior issues, which has a significant positive impact on workplace culture overall.

> **People are pretty much alike. Its only that our differences are more susceptible to definition than our similarities.**
>
> Linda Ellerbee

1

"Civilization is the process in which one gradually increases the number of people included in the term 'we' or 'us' and, at the same time, decreases those labelled 'you' or 'them' until that category has no-one left in it."

Howard Winters

NEXT STEPS

Congratulations! You have now completed this Learning Short-take® title. The entire list of Learning Short-takes® can be found on the TPC website.

In this section we have suggested Learning Short-take® titles for you that will build your learning. You may order these Learning Short-takes® online at www.tpc.net.au or from your bookstores.

The Effective Leader
Skills and Tools for Inspired Leadership

Learning Short-take® Outline

The Effective Leader will guide managers and leaders at all levels towards maximizing your effectiveness as a leader in the workplace. By demystifying the key concepts of communication, team building, leadership styles, individual and team motivation, performance, and interpersonal skills, you will be better equipped for success in your leadership role.

The Effective Leader includes covers both the essential theory and practical skills for successful leadership of teams. Through a series of self-assessment and action learning activities you will identify the differences between management and leadership, write a vision and mission statements, and identify your natural leadership style. **The Effective Leader** will illustrate how to use additional leadership styles and how to plan and lead effective team meetings.

Increased leadership skills moves individuals and teams to increased resilience in the face of change, enhanced performance and greater success!

The Effective Leader includes the **Meeting Planner** and **Meeting Agenda**, provided as free downloadable tools.

Learning Objectives

- Define of the relationship between leadership and management.
- Understand the meaning of vision, mission and values.
- Know the role of leader as coach.
- Apply the theory of the functional and situational approaches to leadership.
- Work on the personal qualities of leadership and to display the will to lead.
- Have a high regard for communication in the leadership process and to develop the ability to communicate.
- List ways to influence motivation for each member of your team.

Course Content

- Part 1: Principles of Effective Leadership
- Part 2: Management vs Leadership
- Part 3: Leadership & Vision
- Part 4: Leadership & Mission
- Part 5: Leadership Style
- Part 6: Understanding Behavior
- Part 7: Leadership & the Theory of Roles
- Part 8: Leading a Team
- Part 9: Managing Team Meetings
- Part 10: Personal and Group Motivation

Making Meetings Work
Getting the Most out of Meetings

Course Content

- Part 1: Types of Meetings
- Part 2: Why Meetings Fail
- Part 3: Solutions to Meeting Barriers
- Part 4: Planning the Meeting
- Part 5: Preparing the Agenda
- Part 6: Conducting the Meeting

Learning Short-take® Outline

Making Meetings Work combines self-study with realistic workplace activities to provide you with the key skills and techniques to make meetings work. Your meetings will become more focused, efficient, targeted and more likely to have a productive impact on the company's bottom-line. You will learn how to more effectively prepare, manage, facilitate and actively participate in meetings.

It is estimated that the average professional spends 61.5 hours per month in meetings, or two weeks every year. It is also estimated that at least 50% of this time is wasted in unproductive meeting activity. **Making Meetings Work** will provide you with the tools to help you save time and money.

Making Meetings Work includes the **Meeting Administration Checklist, Meeting Agenda** and **Meeting Minutes** provided as free downloadable tools.

Learning Objectives

- Evaluate your current level of meeting success.
- Identify the various types of meetings and explain key differences.
- Develop solutions to common meeting problems.
- Outline the steps for a successful meeting.
- Carry out meeting planning and preparation.
- Create a Skill Development Action Plan.

Listen and Be Listened To
Get Inside the Customer's Mind

Learning Short-take® Outline
combines self-study with realistic workplace activities to provide you with the key skills and techniques of effective and enhanced listening. You will learn to build more effective work relationships with your co-workers and leaders by tuning into key communication messages and responding appropriately. You will learn tips, tricks and techniques to boost active listening capability and discover that effective listening helps command respect from both the speakers and listeners point of view.

Our unique view of the world and personal style - based on our values, beliefs, attitudes and behaviors - affects how we act, perceive information, and communicate with others. It also influences the way we listen and how others listen to us. When we expect to hear certain things, we may pay attention to only what interests us. Our perception about a person, situation or subject influences our reception of information, and how much attention we choose to pay. **Listen and Be Listened To** breaks down the art and skill of active listening which is critical to building and maintaining effective working relationships.

Listen and Be Listened To includes an impactful 'Listening Tips' Wall Chart, provided to you as a free download.

Learning Objectives
- Define listening.
- Explain why listening is important.
- Identify the barriers to effective listening.
- Identify their listening style and the listening style of others.
- Demonstrate techniques for active listening.
- Create a Skill Development Action Plan.

Course Content
- Part 1: Listening & Communication
- Part 2: Listening versus Hearing
- Part 3: Barriers to Effective Listening
- Part 4: Your Natural Listening Style
- Part 5: Passive Listening
- Part 6: Active Listening
- Part 7: Better Questions, Better Answers

TPC - The Performance Company is known world wide as 'the place to go' for Corporate Training Courses, e-Learning, Train the Trainer and Instructional Design Programs.

Corporate Training Division

> Global Learning Platform - Coordinate your training worldwide
> Instructional Design - Customized instructor-led and e-Learning courses for your organization
> Trainer Development - Maximize your training effectiveness
> Coaching - Get the best from your participants
> Strategic Consulting - Helping clients meet their goals

Learning Short-takes® Division

> Professional Development
> Sales and Customer Service
> Leadership and Management
> Trainer Development
> Able to be customized for individual clients

www.tpc.net.au